PENGUIN BOOKS

Selected Poems: Roger McGough

Roger McGough is one of Britain's best-known poetry voices. Following the success of the bestselling Penguin collection *The Mersey Sound* (with Brian Patten and the late Adrian Henri), he has been captivating children and adults alike with his unique blend of heart and wit for more than four decades. Much travelled and translated, he is now an international ambassador for poetry, and was awarded a CBE for services to literature in 2004. In 2001 he was honoured with the Freedom of the City of Liverpool.

D0321258

Selected Poems

ROGER McGOUGH

PENGUIN BOOKS

PENGUIN BOOKS

Published by the Penguin Group
Penguin Books Ltd, 80 Strand, London WC2R ORL, England
Penguin Group (USA), Inc., 375 Hudson Street, New York, New York 10014, USA
Penguin Group (Canada), 90 Eglinton Avenue East, Suite 700, Toronto, Ontario, Canada M4P 2Y3
(a division of Pearson Penguin Canada Inc.)
Penguin Ireland, 25 St Stephen's Green, Dublin 2, Ireland (a division of Penguin Books Ltd)
Penguin Group (Australia), 250 Camberwell Road, Camberwell, Victoria 3124, Australia
(a division of Pearson Australia Group Pty Ltd)
Penguin Books India Pvt Ltd, 11 Community Centre,
Panchsheel Park, New Delhi – 110 017, India
Penguin Group (NZ), cnr Airborne and Rosedale Roads, Albany
Auckland 1310, New Zealand (a division of Pearson New Zealand Ltd)
Penguin Books (South Africa) (Pty) Ltd, 24 Sturdee Avenue,
Rosebank, Johannesburg 2196, South Africa

Penguin Books Ltd, Registered Offices: 80 Strand, London WC2R ORL, England

www.penguin.com

This selection first published in Penguin Books 2006
1

'Love in the Laundrette' was commissioned by Derbyshire County Council
for the Literature Festival 2006

Set by Rowland Phototypesetting Ltd, Bury St Edmunds, Suffolk
Printed in England by Clays Ltd, St Ives plc

ISBN–10: 0–141–02322–8
ISBN–13: 978–0–141–02322–9

Contents

Pay-back Time

O Lord, let me be a burden on my children
For long, they've been a burden upon me.
May they fetch and carry, clean and scrub
And do so cheerfully.

Let them take it in turns at putting me up.
Nice, sunny rooms at the top of the stairs
With a walk-in bath and lift installed
At great expense.   Theirs.

Insurance against the body-blows of time
Isn't that what having children's all about?
To bring them up knowing that they owe you
And can't contract out?

What is money for but to spend on their schooling?
Designer clothes, mindless hobbies, usual stuff.
Then as soon as they're earning, off they go.
Well, enough's enough.

It's been a blessing watching them develop
The parental pride we felt as each one grew
But Lord, let me be a burden on my children.
And on my children's children too.

Learning to Read

Learning to read during the war
wasn't easy, as books were few
and far between. But Mother
made sure I didn't go to sleep
without a bedtime story.

Because of the blackout
the warm, comforting glow
of a bedside lamp was not permitted.
So Mum would pull back the curtains
and open wide the window.

And by the light of a blazing factory
or a crashed Messerschmitt,
cuddled up together, she would read
saucebottles, jamjars, and, my
all-time favourite, a tin of Ovaltine.

So many years ago, but still
I remember her gentle guidance
as I read aloud my first sentence:
'S-p-r-i-n-k-l-e t-w-o h-e-a-p-e-d
t-e-a-s-p-o-o-n-s-f-u-l o-f ...

My Little Eye

The cord of my new dressing-gown
he helps me tie

Then on to my father's shoulder
held high

The world at night with my little eye
I spy

The moon close enough to touch
I try

Silver-painted elephants have learned
to fly

Giants fence with searchlights
in the sky

Too soon into the magic shelter
he and I

Air raids are so much fun
I wonder why

In the bunk below, a big boy
starts to cry.

Snipers

When I was kneehigh to a tabletop,
Uncle Ted came home from Burma.
He was the youngest of seven brothers
so the street borrowed extra bunting
and whitewashed him a welcome.

All the relations made the pilgrimage,
including us, laughed, sang, made a fuss.
He was as brown as a chairleg,
drank tea out of a white mug the size of my head,
and said next to nowt.

But every few minutes he would scan
the ceiling nervously, hands begin to shake.
'For snipers,' everyone later agreed,
'A difficult habit to break.'

Sometimes when the two of us were alone,
he'd have a snooze after dinner
and I'd keep an eye open for Japs.
Of course, he didn't know this
and the tanner he'd give me before I went
was for keeping quiet,
but I liked to think it was money well spent.

Being Uncle Ted's secret bodyguard
had its advantages, the pay was good
and the hours were short, but even so,
the novelty soon wore off, and instead,
I started school and became an infant.

Later, I learned that he was in a mental home.
'Needn't tell anybody . . . Nothing serious
. . . Delayed shock . . . Usual sort of thing
. . . Completely cured now the doctors say.'
The snipers came down from the ceiling
but they didn't go away.

Over the next five years they picked off
three of his brothers; one of whom was my father.
No glory, no citations,
Bang! straight through the heart.

Uncle Ted's married now, with a family.
He doesn't say much, but each night after tea,
he still dozes fitfully in his favourite armchair.
He keeps out of the sun, and listens now and then
for the tramp tramp tramp of the Colonel Bogeymen.
He knows damn well he's still at war,
just that the snipers aren't Japs any more.

Tramp Tramp Tramp

Insanity left him when he needed it most.
Forty years at Bryant & May, and a scroll
To prove it. Gold lettering, and a likeness
Of the Founder. Grandad's name writ small:
'William McGarry, faithful employee'.

A spent match by the time I knew him.
Choking on fish bones, talking to himself,
And walking round the block with a yardbrush
Over his shoulder. 'What for, Gran?' 'Hush . . .
Poor man, thinks he's marching off to war.

'Spitting image of Charlie, was your Grandad,
And taller too.' She'd sigh, 'Best-looking
Man in Seaforth. And straight-backed?
Why, he'd walk down Bridge Road
As if he had a coat-hanger in his suit.'

St Joseph's Hospice for the Dying
Is where Chaplin made his last movie.
He played Grandad, and gave a fine performance
Of a man raging against God, and cursing
The nuns and nurses who tried to hold him down.

Insanity left him when he needed it most.
The pillow taken from his face
At the moment of going under. Screaming
And fighting to regain the years denied,
His heart gave out, his mind gave in, he died.

The final scene brings tears to everybody's eyes.
In the parlour, among suppurating candles
And severed flowers, I see him smiling
Like I'd never seen him smile before.
Coat-hanger at his back. Marching off to war.

Hearts and Flowers

Aunty Marge,
Spinster of the parish, never had a boyfriend.
Never courted, never kissed.
A jerrybuilt dentist and a smashed jaw
Saw to that.

To her,
Life was a storm in a holy-water font
Across which she breezed
With all the grace and charm
Of a giraffe learning to windsurf.

But sweating
In the convent laundry, she would iron
Amices, albs and surplices
With such tenderness and care
You'd think priests were still inside.

Deep down,
She would like to have been a nun
And talked of missing her vocation
As if it were the last bus home:
'It passed me by when I was looking the other way.'

'Besides,'
She'd say, 'What Order would have me?
The Little Daughters of the Woodbine?
The Holy Whist Sisters?' A glance at the ceiling.
'He's not that hard up.'

We'd laugh
And protest, knowing in our hearts that He wasn't.
But for the face she would have been out there,
Married, five kids, another on the way.
Celibacy a gift unearned, unasked for.

But though
A goose among grown-ups,
Let loose among kids
She was an exploding fireworks factory,
A runaway pantomime horse.

Everybody's
Favourite aunt. A cuddly toy adult
That sang loud and out of tune.
That dropped, knocked over and bumped into things,
That got ticked off just like us.

                                        Next to
A game of cards she liked babysitting best.
Once the parents were out of the way
It was every child for itself. In charge,
Aunt Marge, renegade toddler-in-chief.

                                        Falling
Asleep over pontoon, my sister and I,
Red-eyed, would beg to be taken to bed.
'Just one more game of snap,' she'd plead,
And magic two toffees from behind an ear.

                                    Then suddenly
Whooshed upstairs in the time it takes
To open the front door. Leaving us to possum,
She'd tiptoe down with the fortnightly fib:
'Still fast asleep, not a murmur all night. Little angels.'

                                        But angels
Unangelic, grew up and flew away. And fallen,
Looked for brighter toys. Each Christmas sent a card
With kisses, and wondered how she coped alone.
Up there in a council flat. No phone.

                    Her death
Was as quick as it was clumsy. Neighbours
Found the body, not us. Sitting there for days
Stiff in Sunday best. Coat half-buttoned, hat askew.
On her way to Mass. Late as usual.

                         Her rosary
Had snapped with the pain, the decades spilling,
Black beads trailing. The crucifix still
Clenched in her fist. Middle finger broken.
Branded into dead flesh, the sign of the cross.

                     From the missal
In her lap, holy pictures, like playing cards,
Lay scattered. Five were face-up:
A Full House of Sacred Hearts and Little Flowers.
Aunty Marge, lucky in cards.

Casablanca

You must remember this
To fall in love in Casablanca
To be the champion of Morocco.

The size of tuppence
Photographs show Uncle Bill holding silver cups
Wearing sepia silks and a George Formby grin.

Dominique
Had silent film star looks. With brown eyes
Black hair and lips full to the brim, she was a race apart.

He brought her over
To meet the family early on. An exotic bloom
In bleak post-war Bootle. Just the once.

Had there been children
There might have been more contact. But letters,
Like silver cups, were few and far between.

At seventy-eight
It's still the same old story. Widowed and lonely
The prodigal sold up and came back home.

I met him that first Christmas
He spoke in broken scouse. Apart from that
He looked like any other bow-legged pensioner.

He had forgotten the jockey part
The fight for love and glory had been a brief episode
In a long, and seemingly, boring life.

It turned out
He had never felt at home there
Not a week went by without him thinking of Liverpool.

Casablanca
The airplane on the runway. She in his arms.
Fog rolling in from the Mersey. As time goes by.

Bye Bye Black Sheep

Volunteering at seventeen, Uncle Joe
Went to Dunkirk as a Royal Marine
And lived, not to tell the tale.
Demobbed, he brought back a broken 303,
A quiver of bayonets, and a kitbag
Of badges, bullets and swastikas
Which he doled out among warstruck nephews.

With gasflame-blue eyes and dark unruly hair
He could have been God's gift. Gone anywhere.
But a lifetime's excitement had been used up
On his one-and-only trip abroad. Instead,
Did the pools and horses. 'Lash me, I'm bored,'
He'd moan, and use language when Gran
Was out of the room. He was our hero.

But not for long. Apparently he was
No good. Couldn't hold down a job.
Gave the old buck to his Elders and Betters.
Lazy as sin, he turned to drink
And ended up marrying a Protestant.
A regular black sheep was Uncle Joe.
Funny how wrong kids can be.

What Happened to Henry

What happened to Henry Townsend that summer
still turns my stomach. Not long after the war
when barrage balloons had been cut loose
and coal was delivered by horse and cart

lads would chase the wagon up the street
and when the coalie wasn't looking
grab hold of the tailboard, and legs dangling
hang there for as long as they could.

According to one, Henry, head thrown back
and swinging too close to the edge,
had caught his foot between the spokes
of the rear left wheel. As it turned

his leg snapped in half. I heard the screams
three streets away. Not his, but his mother's,
who'd been gabbing on the corner.
Air-raid sirens to send us all scurrying.

The driver, ashen-faced beneath the coaldust
held fast the reins to prevent the horse
from moving, but nervous, it bucked
and strained and tried to pull away.

Glad to be of use, two men unbuckled the traces,
freed the horse and laid the shafts gently down.
A kitchen chair was brought out so that
Henry could take the weight off his leg.

                    *   *   *

Those are the facts and this is the picture:
Late one summer's afternoon in Seaforth
on a wooden chair on a cobbled street
a ten-year-old sits with his leg in a wheel.

His mother is crying, but not Henry.
He is stock-still. Against her blue pinny
his face has the pale luminescence of an angel.
A neighbour brings him out a drink of water,

cup and saucer, best china. No sign yet
of an ambulance. Not a policeman in sight.
Frantic, my gran arrives to chase me home.
(Compared to his sister, though, Henry got off light.)

What Happened to Dorothy

That's me on the left.
Page-boy in a velvet suit.
Four years old, blond curls and scowling.
Lucky horseshoe trailing.

That's Dorothy, Maid-of-Honour.
Though only three years older,
in her long white dress,
veil and floral tiara
she could be a teenager.

She never would be, though.

(It wasn't a road accident)
    Tin bath in the kitchen.
(It wasn't diphtheria)
    Pan after pan of boiling water.
(Or polio, or cancer)
    Kids warned not to run about.
(It wasn't murder on the sand dunes)
    Only half full, but scalding
(It wasn't drowning in the canal)
    When she tripped and fell in.

That's me on the left.
Lucky horseshoe still trailing.
That's Dorothy, still seven.

The Railings

You came to watch me playing cricket once.
Quite a few of the fathers did.
At ease, outside the pavilion
they would while away a Saturday afternoon.
Joke with the masters, urge on
their flannelled offspring. But not you.

Fielding deep near the boundary
I saw you through the railings.
You were embarrassed when I waved
and moved out of sight down the road.
When it was my turn to bowl though
I knew you'd still be watching.

Third ball, a wicket, and three more followed.
When we came in at the end of the innings
the other dads applauded and joined us for tea.
Of course, you had gone by then. Later,
you said you'd found yourself there by accident.
Just passing. Spotted me through the railings.

* * *

Speech-days • Prize-givings • School-plays
The Twentyfirst • The Wedding • The Christening
You would find yourself there by accident.
Just passing. Spotted me through the railings.

Squaring Up

When I was thirteen and crimping my first quiff
Dad bought me a pair of boxing-gloves
In the hope that I would aspire to the Noble Art.

But I knew my limitations from the start:
Myopia, cowardice and the will to come second.
But I feigned enthusiasm for his sake.

Straight after tea, every night for a week
We would go a few rounds in the yard.
Sleeves rolled up, collarless and gloveless

He would bob and weave and leave me helpless.
Uppercuts would tap me on the chin
Left hooks muss my hair, haymakers tickle my ear.

Without glasses, only one thing was clear:
The fact that I was hopeless. He had a son
Who couldn't square up. So we came to blows.

Losing patience, he caught me on the nose.
I bled obligingly. A sop. A sacrifice.
Mum threw in the towel and I quit the ring.

But when the bell goes each birthday I still feel the sting
Not of pain, but of regret. You said sorry
And you were. I didn't. And I wasn't.

Sacrifices

I was forever hearing about the sacrifices
My parents made.
Little ones almost daily
Big ones when required.

Having me meant sacrifices. Going without.
And then to cap it all, the Scholarship:
School uniforms, violin lessons,
Elocution, extra tuition.

'If it's not one thing it's another.
I hope you're worth it.' But was I?
The dictionary confirmed my doubts:
'*Sacrifice*, a ritual killing of a person
or animal with the intention of pleasing a deity.'

Sacrifice. No, I wasn't worth it.
All that blood for a few O-levels.

Wearing Thin

'You'll soon grow into it,' she would say
When buying a school blazer three sizes too big.
And she was right as mothers usually are.

Syrup of figs. Virol. Cod liver oil.
Within a year I did grow into it
By then, of course, it was threadbare.

Pulling in different directions
My clothes and I never matched.
And in changing-rooms nothing has changed.

I can buy what I like and when,
New clothes that are a perfect fit.
Full-length mirror, nervous grin,
It's me now that's threadbare, wearing thin.

Snowing Down South

'It's snowing down south,' one girl would say
When another's petticoat showed beneath the skirt
And, giggling, they would rush off to the Ladies.

Modesty restored, they would return to the floor
And dance demurely, with a poise we could not match
We boys, who stood pretending not to watch.

Then half an hour or so before the Last Waltz
The DJ would put on some rock 'n' roll
And emboldened with ale, we'd form a ring.

Eyes closed, they'd spin, those girls, skirts swirling high
To reveal . . . Need I go on? Mid-fifties.
You've seen the pictures, heard the songs.

In the spotlight of our lascivious gaze
Fired by the rhythm, our whistles and screeches
Down south, suddenly, everything is peaches.

'What does your father do?'

At university, how that artful question embarrassed me.
In the common-room, coffee cup balancing on cavalry twills
Some bright spark (usually Sociology) would want an answer.
Shame on me, as feigning lofty disinterest, I would hesitate.

Should I mumble 'docker' in the hope of being misheard?
('There he goes, a doctor's son, and every inch the medical man.')
Or should I pick up the hook and throw it down like a gauntlet?
'Docker. My dad's a docker.' A whistle of corduroy.

How about? 'He's a stevedore, from the Spanish "estibador"
Meaning a packer, or loader, as in ship.' No, sounds too
On the Waterfront, and Dad was no Marlon Brando.
Besides, it's the handle they want not the etymology.

'He's a foreman on the docks.' A hint of status? Possibly.
A touch of class? Hardly. Better go with the straightforward:
'He works on the docks in Liverpool,' which leaves it open.
Crane-driver? Customs and Excise Officer? Canteen manager?

Clerk? Chairman of the Mersey Docks and Harbour Board?
In dreams, I hear him naming the docks he knew and loved.
A mantra of gentle reproach: *Gladstone, Hornby, Alexandra,*
Langton, Brocklebank, Canada, Huskisson, Sandon, Wellington,

Bramley Moor, Nelson, Salisbury, Trafalgar, Victoria.

An Apology

Sincere apologies, too late I know, for not getting engaged
on the night we'd planned, Christmas Eve 1962. I had the ring
in my pocket, the one we'd bought together that November
from the little jewellers on Whitefriargate in Hull. Remember?

After Midnight Mass, arm-in-arming back to ours,
we linger outside the gates of Seaforth Park. The moon
smiling and expectant. No wind, no people, no cars.
Sheets of ice are nailed to the streets with stars.

The scene is set, two lovers on the silver screen.
A pause, the copy-book kiss. Did angels sing?
This was my moment, the cue to pledge my troth,
to take out the blue, velvet box, and do my stuff.

But marriage was a bridge I feared might be detonated,
And I had this crazy idea that if I didn't mention it, then you
wouldn't either. That we'd collude in romantic amnesia.
That life would go on as before. What could be easier?

Christmas passed. Enraged, you blew up. I felt the blast.
We got engaged. It didn't last.

Comeclose and Sleepnow

it is afterwards
and you talk on tiptoe
happy to be part
of the darkness
lips becoming limp
a prelude to tiredness.
Comeclose and Sleepnow
for in the morning
when a policeman
disguised as the sun
creeps into the room
and your mother
disguised as birds
calls from the trees
you will put on a dress of guilt
and shoes with broken high ideals
and refusing coffee
run
alltheway
home.

The Act of Love

The Act of Love lies somewhere
between the belly and the mind
I lost the love sometime ago
Now I've only the act to grind.

Brought her home from a party
don't bother swapping names
identity's not needed
when you're only playing games.

High on bedroom darkness
we endure the pantomime
ships that go bang in the night
run aground on the sands of time.

Saved in the nick of dawn
it's cornflakes and then goodbye
another notch on the headboard
another day wondering why.

The Act of Love lies somewhere
between the belly and the mind
I lost the love sometime ago
Now I've only the act to grind.

May Ball

The evening lay before us
like her silken dress
arranged carefully over the bed.
It would be a night to remember.
We would speak of it often
in years to come. There would
be good food and wine,
cabaret, and music to dance to.
How we'd dance.
How we'd laugh.
We would kiss indiscreetly,
and what are lawns for
but to run barefoot across?

But the evening didn't do
what it was told.
It's the morning after now
and morningafter cold.
I don't know what went wrong
but I blame her. After all
I bought the tickets.
Of course, I make no mention,
that's not my style,
and I'll continue to write
at least for a while.
I carry her suitcase down to the hall,
our first (and her last) University Ball.

Discretion

Discretion is the better part of Valerie
though all of her is nice
lips as warm as strawberries
eyes as cold as ice
the very best of everything
only will suffice
not for her potatoes
and puddings made of rice

Not for her potatoes
and puddings made of rice
she takes carbohydrates
like God takes advice
a surfeit of ambition
is her particular vice
Valerie fondles lovers
like a mousetrap fondles mice

And though in the morning
she may whisper: 'it was nice'
you can tell by her demeanour
that she keeps her love on ice
but you've lost your hardearned heart
now you'll have to pay the price

for she'll kiss you on the memory
and vanish in a trice

Valerie is corruptible
but known to be discreet
Valerie rides a silver cloud
where once she walked the street.

You and Your Strange Ways

increasingly oftennow
you reach into your handbag
(the one I bought some xmasses ago)
and bringing forth
a pair of dead cats
skinned and glistening
like the undersides of tongues
or old elastoplasts
sticky with earwigs
you hurl them at my eyes
and laugh cruellongly
why?
even though we have grown older together
and my kisses are little more than functional
i still love you
you and your strange ways

Vinegar

sometimes
i feel like a priest
in a fish & chip queue
quietly thinking
as the vinegar runs through
how nice it would be
to buy supper for two

My cat and i

Girls are simply the prettiest things
My cat and i believe
And we're always saddened
When it's time for them to leave

We watch them titivating
(that often takes a while)
And though they keep us waiting
My cat & i just smile

We like to see them to the door
Say how sad it couldn't last
Then my cat and i go back inside
And talk about the past.

The Cats' Protection League

Midnight. A knock at the door.
Open it? Better had.
Three heavy cats, mean and bad.

They offer protection. I ask, 'What for?'
The Boss-cat snarls, 'You know the score.
Listen man and listen good

If you wanna stay in the neighbourhood.
Pay your dues or the toms will call
And wail each night on the backyard wall.

Mangle the flowers, and as for the lawn
A smelly minefield awaits you at dawn.'
These guys meant business without a doubt

Three cans of tuna, I handed them out.
They then disappeared like bats into hell
Those bad, bad cats from the CPL.

Mafia Cats

We're the Mafia cats
   Bugsy, Franco and Toni
We're crazy for pizza
   With hot pepperoni

We run all the rackets
   From gambling to vice
On St Valentine's Day
   We massacre mice

We always wear shades
   To show that we're meanies
Big hats and sharp suits
   And drive Lamborghinis

We're the Mafia cats
   Bugsy, Franco and Toni
Love Sicilian wine
   And cheese macaroni

But we have a secret
   (And if you dare tell
You'll end up with the kitten
   At the bottom of the well

Or covered in concrete
  And thrown into the deep
For this is one secret
  You really must keep.)

We're the Cosa Nostra
  Run the scams and the fiddles
But at home we are
  Mopsy, Ginger and Tiddles.

At Lunchtime

When the bus stopped suddenly
to avoid damaging
a mother and child in the road,
the younglady in the green hat sitting opposite
was thrown across me,
and not being one to miss an opportunity
i started to make love.

At first she resisted,
saying that it was too early in the morning
and too soon after breakfast,
and anyway, she found me repulsive.
But when i explained
that this being a nuclearage
the world was going to end at lunchtime,
she took off her green hat,
put her busticket into her pocket
and joined in the exercise.

The buspeople,
and there were many of them,
were shockedandsurprised,
and amusedandannoyed.

But when word got around
that the world was going to end at lunchtime,
they put their pride in their pockets
with their bustickets
and made love one with the other.
And even the busconductor,
feeling left out,
climbed into the cab
and struck up some sort of relationship with the driver.

That night, on the bus coming home,
we were all a little embarrassed,
especially me and the younglady in the green hat,
and we all started to say
in different ways
how hasty and foolish we had been.
But then, always having been a bitofalad,
i stood up and said it was a pity
that the world didnt nearly end every lunchtime,
and that we could always pretend.
And then it happened ...

Quick asa crash
we all changed partners,
and soon the bus was aquiver
with white, mothball bodies doing naughty things.

And the next day
And everyday
In everybus
In everystreet
In everytown
In everycountry

People pretended
that the world was coming to an end at lunchtime.
It still hasnt.
Although in a way it has.

On Picnics

at the goingdown of the sun
and in the morning
i try to remember them
but their names are ordinary names
and their causes are thighbones
tugged excitedly from the soil
by frenchchildren
on picnics

A Square Dance

In Flanders fields in Northern France
They're all doing a brand new dance
It makes you happy and out of breath
And it's called the Dance of Death

Everybody stands in line
Everybody's feeling fine
We're all going to a hop
1 – 2 – 3 and over the top

It's the dance designed to thrill
It's the mustard gas quadrille
A dance for men – girls have no say in it
For your partner is a bayonet

See how the dancers sway and run
To the rhythm of the gun
Swing your partner dos-y-doed
All around the shells explode

Honour your partner form a square
Smell the burning in the air
Over the barbed wire kicking high
Men like shirts hung out to dry

If you fall that's no disgrace
Someone else will take your place
'Old soldiers never die ...'
                    ... Only young ones

In Flanders fields where mortars blaze
They're all doing the latest craze
Khaki dancers out of breath
Doing the glorious Dance of Death
Doing the glorious Dance of Death

Let me Die a Youngman's Death

Let me die a youngman's death
not a clean & inbetween
the sheets holywater death
not a famous-last-words
peaceful out of breath death

When I'm 73
& in constant good tumour
may I be mown down at dawn
by a bright red sports car
on my way home
from an allnight party

Or when I'm 91
with silver hair
& sitting in a barber's chair
may rival gangsters
with hamfisted tommyguns burst in
& give me a short back & insides

Or when I'm 104
& banned from the Cavern
may my mistress
catching me in bed with her daughter
& fearing for her son
cut me up into little pieces
& throw away every piece but one

Let me die a youngman's death
not a free from sin tiptoe in
candle wax & waning death
not a curtains drawn by angels borne
'what a nice way to go' death.

I am not Sleeping

I don't want any of that
'We're gathered here today
to celebrate his life, not mourn his passing.'
Oh yes you are. Get one thing straight,
You're not here to celebrate
but to mourn until it hurts.

I want wailing and gnashing of teeth.
I want sobs, and I want them uncontrollable.
I want women flinging themselves on the coffin
and I want them inconsolable.

Don't dwell on my past but on your future.
For what you see is what you'll be,
and sooner than you think.
So get weeping. Fill yourselves with dread.
For I am not sleeping. I am dead.

You and I

I explain quietly. You
hear me shouting. You
try a new tack. I
feel old wounds reopen.

You see both sides. I
see your blinkers. I
am placatory. You
sense a new selfishness.

I am a dove. You
recognize the hawk. You
offer an olive branch. I
feel the thorns.

You bleed. I
see crocodile tears. I
withdraw. You
reel from the impact.

40 — Love

middle	aged
couple	playing
ten	nis
when	the
game	ends
and	they
go	home
the	net
will	still
be	be
tween	them

No Message

At first, picture postcards.
Next to my address:
A blank stare

The occasional letter.
Envelope torn open to reveal:
An empty page

The late-night phone call.
I recognize the intake of your breath
But no voice

Finally, the bottle
Washed up on the beach
by the morning tide

Pulling out the cork
I remove the slip of paper.
In your handwriting it says:

'No Message.'

A Golden Life

We live a simple life
my wife and I. Are
the envy of our friends.
We are artists. Skilled craftsmen.
I am good with my hands
She with hers.
I am a goldsmith
She a masseuse.

I design and make
gold lockets that cannot be opened
necklaces that will not fasten
ornate keys for which there are no locks.
Trinkets to buy and hoard
toys for the rich and bored.
Things useless, but beautiful.

Compared with the objects I make,
I am dull.
My wife is not dull,
She is exciting.
After a hard day at the parlour
or visiting hotels
(I do not pry)
She comes home
tired, but exciting.

I give her something golden
each evening something new.
It makes her smile.
She rewards me with her golden body
which I melt and shape at will.
Fashioning, with consummate skill,
the precious metal of her flesh.

We live a golden life
my wife and I. Dream
golden dreams. And
each golden morning
go our golden ways.
Make golden dreams for strangers.
Golden nights
and golden days.

The Rot

Some years ago the Rot set in.
It began in a corner of the bedroom
following the birth of the second child.
It spread into the linen cupboard
and across the fabric of our lives.
Experts came to treat it.
Could not.
The Rot could not be stopped.

Dying now, we live with it.
The fungus grows.
It spreads across our faces.
We watch the smiles rot,
gestures crumble.
Diseased, we become the disease.
Part of the fungus.
The part that dreams. That feels pain.

We are condemned.
Things dying, that flaunt their dying,
that cannot hide, are demolished.
We will rot eachother no longer.
From the street outside
comes the sound of the drill,
as men, hungry for dust,
close in for the kill.

Head Injury

I do not smile because I am happy.
Because I gurgle I am not content.
I feel in colours, mottled, mainly black.
And the only sound I hear is the sea
Pounding against the white cliffs of my skull.

For seven months I lay in a coma.
Agony.
Darkness.
My screams drowned by the wind
Of my imperceptible breathing.

One morning the wind died down. I awoke.

You are with me now as you are everyday
Seeking some glimmer of recognition
Some sign of recovery. You take my hand.
I try to say: 'I love you.'
Instead I squawk,
Eyes bobbing like dead birds in a watertank.
I try to say: 'Have pity on me, pity on yourself
Put a bullet between the birds.'

Instead I gurgle.
You kiss me then walk out of the room.
I see your back.
I feel a colour coming, mottled, mainly black.

Catching up on Sleep

i go to bed early
to catch up on my sleep
            but my sleep
is a slippery customer
it bobs and weaves
            and leaves
me exhausted. It
side steps my clumsy tackles.
    with ease.   Bed
raggled I drag
myself to my knees.

The sheep are countless
I pretend to snore
yearn for chloroform
or a sock on the jaw
body sweats heart beats
there is Panic in the Sheets
until
as dawn slopes up the stairs
to set me free
unawares
sleep catches up on me.

9 to 5 (or cosy biscuit)

What I wouldn't give for a nine to five.
Biscuits in the right hand drawer,
teabreaks, and typists to mentally undress.

The same faces. Somewhere to hang
your hat and shake your umbrella.
Cosy. Everything in its place.

Upgraded every few years. Hobbies.
Glass of beer at lunchtime
Pension to look forward to.

Two kids. Homeloving wife.
Bit on the side when the occasion arises
H.P. Nothing fancy. Neat semi.

           *   *   *

What I wouldn't give for a nine to five.
Glass of beer in the right hand drawer
H.P. on everything at lunchtime.

The same 2 kids. Somewhere to hang
your wife and shake your bit on the side.
Teabreaks and a pension to mentally undress.

The same semifaces upgraded.
Hobbies every few years, neat typists
in wet macs when the umbrella arises.

What I wouldn't give for a cosy biscuit.

Waving at Trains

Do people who wave at trains
Wave at the driver, or at the train itself?
Or, do people who wave at trains
Wave at the passengers? Those hurtling strangers,
The unidentifiable flying faces?

They must think we like being waved at.
Children do perhaps, and alone
In a compartment, the occasional passenger
Who is himself a secret waver at trains.
But most of us are unimpressed.

Some even think they're daft.
Stuck out there in a field, grinning.
But our ignoring them, our blank faces,
Even our pulled tongues and up you signs
Come three miles further down the line.

Out of harm's way by then
They continue their walk.
Refreshed and made pure, by the mistaken belief
That their love has been returned,
Because they have not seen it rejected.

54

It's like God in a way. Another day
Another universe. Always off somewhere.
And left behind, the faithful few,
Stuck out there. Not a care in the world.
All innocence. Arms in the air. Waving.

Unlucky for Some

13 voices from a woman's hostel in Soho, 1979

I

What do I do for a living? Survive.
Simple as that. 'God helps those
who help themselves.' That's what the
vicar told me. So I went into
the supermarket and helped myself.
Got six months. God help those
who help themselves. Nowadays
I'm a traveller. South-west mainly
then back here for the winter.
I like the open air. Plenty of it
and it's free. Everything else I beg
borrow or steal. Keep just about alive.
What do I do for a living? Survive.

2

It runs like duck's water off me back.
What people say. How do they know?
They seem to think I enjoy
looking shabby. Having no money.
Being moved on from cafés,
from warm places. How would
they like it? They'd soon sneer
on the other side of their faces
if they ended up down and out.
Up down and out. Up and down.
Out of luck. That's all you have to be.
Half of them calling the kettle black.
It runs like duck's water off me back.

3

It's the addicts I can't stand.
Getting drunk on pills. Stoned
they call it. Make me sick.
Sticking needles into themselves
in dirty lavatories. Got no shame.
And they get prescriptions. Wish
my doctor would give me one
everytime I felt like a drink.
I could take it along to the
allnight off-licence in Piccadilly
come back here and get drunk
for a week. Get high. Stoned.
It's the addicts I can't stand.

4

I'm no good, that's what I've been told
ever since I can remember. So
I try to live up to my reputation.
Or down to it. Thievin' mainly.
And drugs. You get used to prison.
Don't like it though, being cooped up.
That's why I couldn't work in a shop
or a factory. Drive me crazy.
Can't settle down. 21 years old
and I look 40. It's the drugs.
I'll O.D. probably. Couldn't care less.
Rather die young than grow old.
I'm no good, that's what I've been told.

5

Now I'm one of the idle poor.
A rose in a garden of weeds.
Slightly shrivelled of course, but nevertheless
an interesting species: '*Retrobata Inebriata*'.
I was born into the leisured classes.
No doubt you can tell. Born rich
and married rich as well. Too much
leisure that was the trouble. And drink.
Cost me a husband, home, family.
Now I've only a bed, a roof over my head.
Perhaps I don't deserve more.
I used to be one of the idle rich.
Now I'm one of the idle poor.

6

I get frightened you see. Easily scared.
Trouble is, I know what's goin' on.
The things they've got planned.
The others don't understand, you see.
They say: 'What are you scared of?
There's no need to be frightened.'
I huddle myself up against
the window sometimes. Like a curtain.
Listening to what's goin' on outside.
I've got X-ray hearin', you see.
It stretches for miles. When people
talk about me, I can hear every word.
I get frightened you see. Easily scared.

7

First and foremost I need a coat.
The one I'm wearing's got patches
on the patches. I can't go
for interviews dressed like this.
What sort of a job do you think
I'd get? A job as a tramp?
No thank you. And while I'm here
I need some vests and knickers.
None of them fancy ones either.
And shoes. Two pair. Leather.
Don't argue, I know my rights.
Refuse and I'll take you to court.
First and foremost I need a coat.

8

I try to take up little space.
Keep myself to myself. I find
the best way to get by is to say
nothing. Don't argue, don't interfere.
When there's trouble lie low.
That's why I wear a lot of grey.
Helps me hide away. Blend in
against the background. I eat
very little. Don't smoke or drink.
Get through the day unnoticed
that's the trick. The way to heaven.
Say me prayers each night just in case.
I try to take up little space.

9

It may sound silly but it's true.
I drink like there was no tomorrow
and I can't stand the taste of the stuff.
Never have. My mother was a drunk
and the smell of her was enough.
I drink to forget. I know it's a cliché
but it's true. I drink to forget
and I do. Occasionally I remember
what I was trying not to remember
but by then I've remembered
to drink, in order to make
myself forget. And I do.
It may sound silly but it's true.

10

I would have liked children I suppose.
A family and that. It's natural.
But it's too late now. Too old.
And trouble is I never liked men.
If I'd been born pretty
or with a nice figure, I might
have liked them then. Men,
and sex and that. But I'm
no oil painting. Had to face
that fact right from the start.
And you see, if you're born ugly
well that's the way life goes. But
I would have liked children I suppose.

II

Oh no, I don't have to be here.
I'm not a cast-off like the rest.
I'm one of the lucky ones. I've got
children. Both grown up. A son
and daughter who'd be only too pleased
to have me living with them.
But I prefer my independence.
Besides, they've got their own lives.
I'd only have to pick up the phone
and they'd be over. Or send money.
I mean, I could afford a room
in a nice clean hotel somewhere.
Oh no, I don't have to be here.

12

Things are better now with me new glasses.
I got the last pair just after the war
and I think they'd lost their power.
If I could read I'd be able
to read even better now. Everything's
so much clearer. Faces and places.
Television's improved too. Not
that I'm one for stayin' in.
I prefer to be out and about.
Sightseein' and windowshoppin'.
In and out of the traffic.
If you keep on the move, time soon passes.
Things are better now, with me new glasses.

13

I always wanted to go on the stage.
Dancer mainly, though I had a lovely voice.
Ran away to the bright lights of London
to be a star. Nothing came of it though,
so I went on the game. An actress
of sorts you might say. I'm the oldest
professional in the oldest profession.
Would you like to see me dance?
I'll dance for you. I dance in here
all the time. The girls love it.
Do you like my dancing? Round
and round. Not bad eh? For my age.
I always wanted to go on the stage.

In Transit

She spends her life
in Departure Lounges,
flying from one to another.

Although planes frighten her,
baggage is a bother
and foreigners a bore,

in the stifled hysteria
of an airport
she, in transit, feels secure.

Enjoys the waiting game.
Cheered by storms, strikes
and news of long delays,

among strangers, nervous
and impatient for the off,
the old lady scrambles her days.

The Lesson

A poem that raises the question:
Should there be capital punishment in schools?

Chaos ruled OK in the classroom
as bravely the teacher walked in
the hooligans ignored him
his voice was lost in the din

'The theme for today is violence
and homework will be set
I'm going to teach you a lesson
one that you'll never forget'

He picked on a boy who was shouting
and throttled him then and there
then garrotted the girl behind him
(the one with grotty hair)

Then sword in hand he hacked his way
between the chattering rows
'First come, first severed' he declared
'fingers, feet, or toes'

He threw the sword at a latecomer
it struck with deadly aim
then pulling out a shotgun
he continued with his game

The first blast cleared the backrow
(where those who skive hang out)
they collapsed like rubber dinghies
when the plugs pulled out

'Please may I leave the room sir?'
a trembling vandal enquired
'Of course you may' said teacher
put the gun to his temple and fired

The Head popped a head round the doorway
to see why a din was being made
nodded understandingly
then tossed in a grenade

And when the ammo was well spent
with blood on every chair
Silence shuffled forward
with its hands up in the air

The teacher surveyed the carnage
the dying and the dead
He waggled a finger severely
'Now let that be a lesson' he said.

There Was a Knock on the Door.
It Was the Meat.

There was a knock on the door.
It was the meat. I let it in.
Something freshly slaughtered
Dragged itself into the hall.

Into the living-room it crawled.
I followed. Though headless,
It headed for the kitchen
As if following a scent.

Straight to the oven it went
And lay there. Oozing softly to itself.
Though moved, I moved inside
And opened wide the door.

I switched to Gas Mark Four.
Set the timer. And grasping
The visitor by a stump
Humped it home and dry.

Did I detect a gentle sigh?
A thank you? The thought that I
Had helped a thing in need
Cheered me as I turned up the heat.

Two hours later the bell rang.
It was the meat.

Vegetarians

Vegetarians are cruel, unthinking people.
Everybody knows that a carrot screams when grated.
That a peach bleeds when torn apart.
Do you believe an orange insensitive
to thumbs gouging out its flesh?
That tomatoes spill their brains painlessly?
Potatoes, skinned alive and boiled,
the soil's little lobsters.
Don't tell me it doesn't hurt
when peas are ripped from the scrotum,
the hide flayed off sprouts,
cabbage shredded, onions beheaded.

Throw in the trowel
and lay down the hoe.
Mow no more
Let my people go!

Cabbage

(after 'I like that stuff' by Adrian Mitchell)

Humphrey Bogart died of it
People are terrified of it
> *cancer*
> I hate that stuff

Peter Sellers was laid low with it
one in five of us will go with it
> *heart attack*
> I hate that stuff

Monroe's life turned sour on it
Hancock spent his last half hour on it
> *sleeping pills*
> I hate that stuff

Jimi Hendrix couldn't wait for it
Chemistshops stay open late for it
> *heroin*
> I hate that stuff

Mama Cass choked on it
Blankets get soaked in it
                    vomit
                    I hate that stuff

Women learn to live with it
No one can live without it
                    blood
                    I hate that stuff

Hospitals are packed with it
Saw my mother racked with it
                    pain
                    I hate that stuff

Few like to face the truth of it
We're all living proof of it
                    death
                    I hate that stuff

Schoolkids are forcefed with it
Cattle are served dead with it
                    cabbage
                    I hate that stuff

The Birderman

Most weekends, starting in the spring
Until late summer, I spend angling.
Not for fish. I find that far too tame
But for birds, a much more interesting game.

A juicy worm I use as bait
Cast a line into the tree and wait.
Seldom for long (that's half the fun)
A commotion in the leaves, the job's half done.

Pull hard, jerk home the hook
Then reel him in. Let's have a look . . .
A tiny thing, a fledgling, young enough to spare.
I show mercy. Unhook, and toss it to the air.

It flies nestwards and disappears among the leaves
(What man roasts and braises, he too reprieves).
What next? A magpie. Note the splendid tail.
I wring its neck. Though stringy, it'll pass for quail.

Unlike water, the depths of trees are high
So, standing back, I cast into the sky.
And ledger there beyond the topmost bough,
Until threshing down, like a black cape, screams a crow!

Evil creature! A witch in feathered form.
I try to net the dark, encircling storm.
It caws for help. Its cronies gather round
They curse and swoop. I hold my ground.

An infernal mass, a black, horrific army
I'll not succumb to Satan's origami.
I reach into my coat, I've come prepared,
Bring out my pocket scarecrow – Watch out bird!

It's cross-shaped, the sign the godless fear
In a thunderflap of wings they disappear.
Except of course, that one, ungainly kite
Broken now, and quickly losing height.

I haul it in, and with a single blow
Dispatch it to that Aviary below.
The ebb and flow: magpie, thrush, nightingale and crow.
The wood darkens. Time to go.

I pack away the food I've caught
And thankful for a good day's sport
Amble home. The forest fisherman.
And I'll return as soon as I can

To bird. For I'm a birderer. The birderman.

Honey and Lemon

Jogging around Barnes Common one April morning
when a rat crossed my path twenty metres ahead.
A fat, furry fist spelling danger from the tip
of its pointed nose to the end of its pointing tail.

Dogs daily, magpies frequently, rats? Never.
So, curious, I swerved left into the undergrowth
and took the overgrown path back to where
the beast (it had doubled in size) had scuttled.

Three strides along and there it was, barring
my way like a rival gang of football hooligans.
Red-eyed and snuffling, PLAGUE written all over it.
Motionless, I tried to stifle the fear rising within.

Having read in one of those survival handbooks
that rats love lemon, I spat the honey and lemon
pastille I was sucking straight into the bushes,
and sure enough, the brute dived in after it.

Unfortunately for the rat, a huge grizzly bear,
mad for honey, came crashing through the trees
and tore the creature to pieces with its iron claws.
By then, I was back on the road sprinting for home.

Trees Cannot Name the Seasons

Trees cannot name the seasons
Nor flowers tell the time.
But when the sun shines
And they are charged with light,
They take a day-long breath.
What we call 'night'
Is their soft exhalation.

And when joints creak yet again
And the dead skin of leaves falls,
Trees don't complain
Nor mourn the passing of hours.
What we call 'winter'
Is simply hibernation.

And as continuation
Comes to them as no surprise
They feel no need
To divide and itemize.
Nature has never needed reasons
For flowers to tell the time
Or trees put a name to seasons.

The Lake

For years there have been no fish in the lake.
People hurrying through the park avoid it like the plague.
Birds steer clear and the sedge of course has withered.
Trees lean away from it, and at night it reflects,
not the moon, but the blackness of its own depths.
There are no fish in the lake. But there is life there.
There is life . . .

Underwater pigs glide between reefs of coral debris.
They love it here. They breed and multiply
in sties hollowed out of the mud
and lined with mattresses and bedsprings.
They live on dead fish and rotting things,
drowned pets, plastic and assorted excreta.
Rusty cans they like the best.
Holding them in webbed trotters
their teeth tear easily through the tin
and poking in a snout
they noisily suck out
the putrid matter within.

There are no fish in the lake. But there is life there.
There is life . . .

For on certain evenings after dark
shoals of pigs surface and look out
at those houses near the park.
Where, in bathrooms, children feed stale bread
   to plastic ducks
and in attics, toyyachts have long since runaground.
Where, in livingrooms, anglers dangle their lines
on patterned carpets, and bemoan the fate
of the ones that got away.

Down on the lake, piggy eyes glisten.
They have acquired a taste for flesh.
They are licking their lips. Listen . . .

Fatal Consequences

I don't believe that one about the butterfly –
The air displaced by the fluttering
of its wings in Brazil
causing a tidal wave in Bangladesh.

Mind you,
The day after I shook out
a tablecloth on the patio
there was an earthquake in Mexico.

(Or was it the other way round?)

Ex Patria

After supper, we move out on to the veranda.
Moths flit between lamps. We drink, think about sex
and consider how best to wreck each other's lives.

At the river's edge, the kitchen maids are washing up.
In the age-old tradition, they slap the plates
against the side of a rock, singing tonelessly.

Like tiny chauffeurs, the mosquitoes will soon arrive
and drive us home. O England, how I miss you.
Ascot, Henley, Wimbledon. It's the little things.

Tsutsumu

Tsutsumu: The Japanese art of wrapping items in an
attractive and appropriate way.

Dear Satoshi,
Thank you for the egg. Smashed in transit, I'm afraid.
The origami chicken that it came in, however,
although gooey was exquisite. How clever you are!

We hesitated for ages before gently dismantling
the Taj Mahal. Perhaps now we regret it.
My wife is over the moon with the curry powder.

It seemed a shame to unpick the delicate spinning-wheel.
Straight out of an enchanted castle, we thought!
The plastic thimble will surely come in handy.

The walnut tree was so lifelike
we considered replanting it in our little garden.
Thank you for the walnut.

And that salmon! The magic you weave with paper!
It seemed to shimmer with life and jump for joy.
Sadly the slice of sashumi was well past its sell-by.

When the life-size model of a Toyota Landcruiser
was delivered, we were as tickled as the postman!
Our thanks for the jasmine-scented car-freshener.

Finally, a note of apology.
It was only after we had broken the string,
torn off the paper, and smashed open the box,
that we realized we had destroyed your gift
of a beautiful box. Sorry.

Posh

Where I live is posh
  Sundays the lawns are mown
My neighbours drink papaya squash

Sushi is a favourite nosh
  Each six-year-old has a mobile phone
Where I live is posh

In spring each garden is awash
  with wisteria, pink and fully blown
My neighbours drink papaya squash

Radicchio thrives beneath the cloche
  Cannabis is home grown
Where I live is posh

Appliances by Míele and Bosch
  Sugar-free jam on wholemeal scone
My neighbours drink papaya squash

Birds hum and bees drone
  The paedophile is left alone
My neighbours drink papaya squash
Where I live is posh.

Shite

Where I live is shite
   An inner-city high-rise shack
Social workers shoot on sight

The hospital's been set alight
   The fire brigade's under attack
Where I live is shite

Police hide under their beds at night
   Every road's a cul-de-sac
Social workers shoot on sight

Girls get pregnant just for spite
   My mate's a repo-maniac
Where I live is shite.

Newborn junkies scratch and bite
   Six-year-olds swap sweets for crack
Social workers shoot on sight

Tattooed upon my granny's back
   A fading wrinkled Union Jack
Social workers shoot on sight
Where I live is shite.

The Jogger's Song

After leaving the Harp nightclub in Deptford, a 35-year-old woman was raped and assaulted by two men in Fordham Park. Left in a shocked and dishevelled state she appealed for help to a man in a light-coloured tracksuit who was out jogging. Instead of rescuing her, he also raped her. – *Standard*, 27 January 1984

Well, she was asking for it.
Lying there, cryin out,
dying for it. Pissed of course.
Of course, nice girls don't.
Don't know who she was,
where from, didn't care.
Nor did she. Slut. Slut.

Now I look after myself. Fit.
Keep myself fit. Got
a good body. Good body. Slim.
Go to the gym. Keep in trim.
Girls like a man wiv a good body.
Strong arms, tight arse. Right
tart she was. Slut. Pissed.

Now I don't drink. No fear.
Like to keep a clear
head. Keep ahead. Like
I said, like to know what I'm doin
who I'm screwin (excuse language).
Not like her. Baggage. Half-
dressed, couldn't-care-less. Pissed.

Crawlin round beggin for it.
Lying there, dyin for it.
Cryin. Cryin. Nice girls don't.
Right one she was. A raver.
At night, after dark,
on her own, in the park?
Well, do me a favour.

And tell me this:
If she didn't enjoy it,
why didn't she scream?

End of Story

Sometimes I wish I was back in Nicosia
smoking the wacky-backy with the lads
and watching Sandy getting tarted up.

Night on the town. Blood on the streets.
Razor-blades stitched into the lapels
of his crushed-velvet tartan jacket.

Headcase but funny with it. Not like Fitzy.
Now we're talking nasty bastards.
Four brothers and half a brain between them.

He only knew three questions:
Who are you lookin at? What did you say?
Are you takin the piss?

Simple questions that no one ever got right
because only Fitzy knew the answers:
(a) Beerglass (b) Boot (c) Head-butt.

Put on more charges than the Light Brigade.
Next thing, he marries a local girl.
Maria Somethingopolis. Big name. Big family.

It won't last long, we said. And it didn't.
Took three of them, though. Stabbed him
in the back of a car, then set fire to it.

Cyprus One, England Nil. Mainly, though,
I remember the good times. Sound mates,
cheap bevvy. Moonlight on the Med. End of story.

No Surprises

He wakes when the sun rises
Gets up Exercises
Breakfasts with one whom he despises
Chooses one of his disguises
and his gun Fires his
first bullet It paralyses
Drives into town Terrorizes
Armed police in visors
materialize His demise is
swift No surprises.

Greek Tragedy

Approaching midnight and the mezze unfinished
we linger over Greek coffee and consider
calling for the bill, when suddenly the door
bangs open, and out of the neon-starry sky

falls a dazed giant. He stumbles in
and pinballs his way between the tables
nicking ringlets of deep-fried calamari en route.
Nikos appears from the kitchen, nervous but soothing.

'Double moussaka,' grunts the giant,
'and two bottles of that retsina muck.'
He gazes around the taverna, now freeze-framed.
No tables are empty, but none are full.

You could have broken bits off the silence
and dipped them into your taramasalata.
Then he sees me. I turn to a rubberplant
in the far corner and try to catch its eye,

'Excuse me, can I have the bill, please?'
He staggers over and sits down. The chair groans
and the table shudders. 'I know you, don't I?'
he says. '"Lily the Pink" an' all that crap.

'Give us yer autograph. It's not for me,
it's for me nephew. Stick it on this.'
I sign the crumpled napkin as if it were
the Magna Carta and hand it back.

Then to my girlfriend I say overcheerfully,
'Time we were off, love.' While peering
at the napkin as if I'd blown my nose into it
he threatens: 'Youse are not goin' nowhere.'

On cue, a plate of cheesy mince and two bottles
appear. Flicking our hands from the top of the glasses
he refills them and looks at me hard. Very hard.
'D'ye know who I am?' (I do, but pretend I don't.)

'Eddie Mason. Call me Eddie.' 'Cheers, Eddie.'
'D'ye know what I do?' (I do, but pretend I don't.)
'I'm a villain. Livin' on the edge. Bit like you,
Know what I mean?' (I don't, but pretend I do.)

'I'm in the people business like yourself.'
Lest I am a doubting Thomas, he grabs my hand
and shoves a finger into a dent in his skull.
'Pickaxe. And feel tha' . . . and tha' . . . and tha'.'

Brick, hammer, knife, screwdriver, baseball bat.
He takes me on a guided tour of his scalp.
A map of clubs and pubs, doorways and dives.
Of scores settled and wounds not yet healed.

What he couldn't show me were the two holes
above the left eye, where the bullets went in
a fortnight later. Shot dead in the back of a cab
by the father of a guy whose legs he'd smashed

with an iron bar. He hardly touched
his moussaka, but he ordered more wine.
And it goes without saying, that he shredded
the napkin, and left without paying.

The Terrible Outside

The bus I often took as a boy to visit an aunt
went past it. From the top deck I would look
beyond the wall for signs of life: a rooftop protest,
a banner hung from cell windows. I would picture
the escape. Two men sliding down the rope
and legging it up Walton Vale. Maybe hijacking
the bus and holding us hostage. But I'd talk them
round. Share my sweets and pay their fares.

Years later I am invited there to run a poetry
workshop. An escapism easily contained.
And as I check in and pass through security,
and as door after door clangs open and shut,
I imagine that I am a prisoner. 'But I'm innocent,
I tell you. I was framed.' It's no use protesting,
take the old lag's advice, just keep your head down
and get on with it. The three hours will soon pass.

A class of eighteen. All lifers in their early twenties,
most with tattoos, childishly scratched and inked in.
Nervous, I remove my raincoat and shake my
umbrella. 'It's terrible outside,' I say. Then panic.
'I mean, compared to life inside it's not terrible . . .
It's good. It was the weather I was talking about.
Outside, it's really bad. But not as bad as in here,
of course. Being locked up . . . it must be terrible.'

They look at me blankly, wondering perhaps
if that was my first poem and not thinking much of it.
We talk. I read my stuff and they read theirs.
I answer questions (about fashion and music).
The questions I want to ask I can't. 'Hands up
those who killed their fathers? Hands up
those who killed more than once? Hands up . . .'
But those hands are clean, those faces bright.
Any one of them I'd trust with my life.

Or would I? Time's up and the door clangs open.
They all gather round and insist on shaking my hand.
A hand that touches women, that lifts pints, a hand
that counts money, that buttons up brand-new shirts.
A hand that shakes the hand of the Governor,
that raises an umbrella and waves down a cab.
A hand that trembles and clenches and pushes
itself deep into a raincoat pocket. A hand
that is glad to be part of the terrible outside.

The Identification

So you think it's Stephen?
Then I'd best make sure
Be on the safe side as it were.
Ah, theres been a mistake. The hair
you see, its black, now Stephens fair . . .
Whats that? The explosion?
Of course, burnt black. Silly of me.
I should have known. Then lets get on.

The face, is that the face I ask?
that mask of charred wood
blistered, scarred could
that have been a child's face?
The sweater, where intact, looks
in fact all too familiar.
But one must be sure.

The scoutbelt. Yes thats his.
I recognise the studs he hammered in
not a week ago. At the age
when boys get clothes-conscious
now you know. Its almost
certainly Stephen. But one must
be sure. Remove all trace of doubt.
Pull out every splinter of hope.

Pockets. Empty the pockets.
Handkerchief? Could be any schoolboy's.
Dirty enough. Cigarettes?
Oh this can't be Stephen.
I dont allow him to smoke you see.
He wouldn't disobey me. Not his father.
But thats his penknife. Thats his alright.
And thats his key on the keyring
Gran gave him just the other night.
Then this must be him.

I think I know what happened
. . . . . . about the cigarettes.
No doubt he was minding them
for one of the older boys.
Yes thats it.
Thats him.
Thats our Stephen.

The End of Summer

It is the end of summer
The end of day and cool,
As children, holiday-sated,
Idle happily home from school.

Dusk is slow to gather
The pavements still are bright,
It is the end of summer
And a bag of dynamite

Is pushed behind the counter
Of a department store, and soon
A trembling hand will put an end
To an English afternoon.

The sun on rooftops gleaming
Underlines the need to kill,
It is the end of summer
And all is cool, and still.

It's a Jungle Out There

On leaving the house you'd best say a prayer
Take my advice and don't travel by train
As Tarzan said to Jane, 'It's a jungle out there.'

I'm not a man who will easily scare
But I'd rather chew wasps than get on a plane
On leaving the house you'd best say a prayer.

Give your budgie a cuddle if you dare
'Who's a pretty . . . pathogenic viral strain?'
As Tarzan said to Jane, 'It's a jungle out there.'

Avoid beef like the plague and the sun's blinding glare
Alcopops slowly eat away the brain
On leaving the house you'd best say a prayer

When the sky turns purple better beware
Bacillus on the breeze and acid in the rain
As Tarzan said to Jane, 'It's a jungle out there.'

Don't drink the water and don't breathe the air
For the sake of the children repeat the refrain:
On leaving the house you'd best say a prayer
As Tarzan said to Jane, 'It's a jungle out there.'

A Cautionary Calendar

Beware January,
His greeting is a grey chill.
Dark stranger. First in at the kill.
Get out while you can.

Beware February,
Jolly snowman. But beneath the snow
A grinning skeleton, a scarecrow.
Don't be drawn into that web.

Beware March,
Mad Piper in a many-coloured coat
Who will play a jig then rip your throat.
If you leave home, don't go far.

Beware April,
Who sucks eggs and tramples nests.
From the wind that molests
There is no escape.

Beware May,
Darling scalpel, gall and wormwood.
Scented blossom hides the smell
Of blood. Keep away.

Beware June,
Black lipstick, bruise-coloured rouge,
Sirensong and subterfuge.
    The wide-eyed crazed hypnotic moon.

Beware July,
Its juices overflow. Lover of excess
Overripe in flyblown dress.
    Insatiable and cruel.

Beware August,
The finger that will scorch and blind
Also beckons. The only place you will find
    To cool off is the morgue.

Beware September,
Who speaks softly with honeyed breath.
You promise fruitfulness. But death
    Is the only gift that she'll accept.

Beware October,
Whose scythe is keenest. The old crone
Makes the earth tremble and moan.
    She's mean and won't be mocked.

Beware November,
Whose teeth are sharpened on cemetery stones,
Who will trip you up and crunch your bones.
    Iron fist in iron glove.

    Beware December,
False beard that hides a sneer.
Child-hater. In what year
    Will we know peace?

Poor Old Dead Horses

Don't give your rocking-horse
To the old rag and bony

He'll go straight to the knacker
And haggle for money

The stirrups are torn off
The bridle and harness

Chopped up for firewood
It is thrown on the furnace

And the water that boils
Is chucked down the sluices

To wash away what remains
Of poor old dead horses.

Who Can Remember Emily Frying?

The Grand Old Duke of Wellington
Gave us the wellington boot.
The Earl of Sandwich, so they say,
Invented the sandwich. The suit

Blues saxophonists choose to wear
Is called after Zoot Sims (a Zoot suit).
And the inventor of the saxophone?
Mr Sax, of course. (Toot! Toot!)

And we all recall, no trouble at all,
That buccaneer, long since gone,
Famed for his one-legged underpants –
'Why, shiver me timbers' – Long John.

But who can remember Emily Frying?
(Forgotten, not being a man.)
For she it was who invented
The household frying pan.

And what about Hilary Teapot?
And her cousin, Charlotte Garden-Hose?
Who invented things to go inside birdcages
(You know, for budgies to swing on). Those.

Today is Not a Day for Adultery

Today is not a day for adultery.
The sky is a wet blanket
Being shaken in anger. Thunder
Rumbles through the streets
Like malicious gossip.

Take my advice: braving
The storm will not impress your lover
When you turn up at the house
In an anorak. Wellingtons,
Even coloured, seldom arouse.

Your umbrella will leave a tell-tale
Puddle in the hall. Another stain
To be explained away. Stay in,
Keep your mucus to yourself.
Today is not a day for sin.

Best pick up the phone and cancel.
Postpone until the weather clears.
No point in getting soaked through.
At your age, a fuck's not worth
The chance of catching 'flu.

Your Favourite Hat

Believe me when I tell you that
I long to be your favourite hat

The velvet one. Purply-black
With ribbons trailing at the back

The one you wear to parties, plays,
Assignations on red-letter days

Like a bat in your unlit hall
I'd hang until there came the call

To freedom. To hug your crown
As you set off through Camden Town

To run my fingers through your hair
Unbeknown in Chalcot Square

To let them linger, let them trace
My shadow cast upon your face

Until, on reaching the appointed place
(The pulse at your temple, feel it race!)

Breathless, you whisper: 'At last, at last.'
And once inside, aside I'm cast

There to remain as tick ticks by
Nap rising at each moan and sigh

Ecstatic, curling at the brim
To watch you naked, there with him

Until, too soon, the afternoon gone
You retrieve me, push me on

Then take your leave (as ever, in haste)
Me eager to devour the taste

Of your hair. Your temples now on fire
My tongue, the hatband as you perspire

To savour the dampness of your skin
As you window-gaze. Looking in

But not seeing. Over Primrose Hill
You dawdle, relaxed now, until

Home Sweet Home, where, safely back
Sighing, you impale me on the rack

Is it in spite or because of that
I long to be your favourite hat?

The Map

Wandering lost and lonely in Bologna
I found a street-map on the piazza.
Unfortunately, it was of Verona.

As I was refolding it into a limp concertina,
A voice: 'Ah, you've found it! I'm Fiona,
Let me buy you a spritzer, over there on the terraza.'

Two spritzers later we ordered some pasta
(Bolognese, of course, then zabaglione).
I felt no remorse, merely amore.

Proposing a toast to love at first sight
We laughed and talked over a carafe of chianti
When out of the night, like a ghost, walked my aunty.

'Look who's here,' she cried. 'If if isn't our Tony,
Fancy bumping into you in Italy,
With a lady friend too,' then added, bitterly:

'How are Lynda and the kids? I'm sure they're OK.
While the mice are at home the tomcat will play.'
A nod to Fiona, 'Nice to meet you. Ciao!'

I snapped my grissini. 'Stupid old cow!'
Then turned to Fiona. She was no longer there.
Our romance in tatters, like the map on her chair.

It's Only a P . . .

Feeling a trifle smug after breaking off an untidy,
Drawn-out affair with somebody I no longer fancied
I was strolling through Kensington Gardens
When who should I bump into but Gavin.

Gavin, I should point out, is the husband.
'I'm worried about Lucy,' he said, straight out.
'I don't blame you,' I thought, but said nothing.
'Suspect she's having an affair. Any ideas?'

'Divorce,' I suggested. 'You might even get custody.'
'No, I mean Lucy,' he persisted. 'Who with?'
We walked on in silence, until casually, I asked:
'An affair, you say, what makes you so convinced?'

He stopped and produced from an inside pocket
A sheet of paper which I recognized at once.
It was this poem. Handwritten, an early draft.
Then I saw the gun, 'For God's sake, Gavin,
                                        It's only a p . . .'

Love in the Laundrette

Two of a kind, we have so much in common
I thought, as I cycled past her on the Common

Our bags were stuffed with soiled belongings
Was she lonely too? Filled with untold longings?

I could write a tune, a poem or a play for her
Knowing that soon I would make a play for her

Although our eyes had met only moments ago
Once inside, I decided to give it a go

Cried: 'Let's put our clothes into the same wash!'
The look of horror told me that it wouldn't wash

'Let's save time and money. Share our washing powder.'
But she turned her back and snapped, 'Take a powder.'

She needed her own machine. To run her own cycle.
So I unloaded, and lonely, rode home on my cycle.

This be Another Verse

They don't fuck you up, your mum and dad
(Despite what Larkin says)
It's other grown-ups, other kids
Who, in their various ways

Die. And their dying casts a shadow
Numbering all our days
And we try to keep from going mad
In multifarious ways.

And most of us succeed, thank God,
So if, to coin a phrase
You're fucked up, don't blame your mum and dad
(Despite what Larkin says).

Blazing Fruit

(or The Role of the Poet as Entertainer)

During dinner the table caught fire.
No one alluded to the fact
and we ate on, regardless of
the flames singeing our conversation.

Unaware of the smoke
and the butlers swooning,
topics ranged from Auden
to Zeffirelli. I was losing
concentration however, and being
short on etiquette, became tense
and began to fidget with the melting cutlery.

I was fashioning a spoon
into a question mark
when the Chablis began to steam
and bubble. I stood up,
mumbled something about having left the gas running
and fled blushing
across the plush terrain of the carpet.
The tut-tut-tutting could be heard above
the cra-cra-cracking of the bone china.

Outside, I caught a cab
to the nearest bus stop.
While, back at the table,
they were toying with blazing fruit
and discussing the Role of the Poet as Entertainer,
when the roof fell in.

An Ordinary Poetry Reading

Tonight will be an ordinary poetry reading
A run-of-the-mill kind of affair
Nothing that will offend or challenge
No *language* as far as I'm aware.

The poets are thoroughly decent
All vetted by our committee
We had hoped Wendy Cope might appear
But she's tied up more's the pity.

And that other one, whose name I forget . . .
Quite famous . . . Recently died . . .
He'd have been good. But never mind,
At least we can say that we tried.

Personally, I prefer actors
Reading the Great Works of the Past
The trouble with poets is they mumble
Get nervous, and then speaktoofast.

And alcohol is a danger
So that's been kept well out of sight
As long as they're sober this evening
They can drink themselves legless all night.

By the way, they've come armed with slim volumes
Which of course, they're desperate to sell
Otherwise, there's coffee in the foyer
With KitKats and Hobnobs as well.

Well, I think that covers everything
All that remains for me to say
Is to wish you ... an ordinary evening
Such a pity I'm unable to stay.

The Logic of Meteors

August in Devon and all is rain. A soft rain
that seems, not to fall from the sky, but to rise
from the ground and drape itself over the trees
and hedgerows like a swirl of silver taffeta.
But I am not interested in matters meteorological.
Not for me the logic of meteors, but the logic of metre.
For this is a Poetry Course and I am the Tutor.

Last night I had a visitor. (Not a female student:
'I'm having trouble with my sestina' ... 'Do come in ...')
But a monster that kamikazied around the room
before ensnaring itself within the vellum lampshade.
Waiting until the moth, light-headed, went into free fall
I clumped it with Ted Hughes' *Birthday Letters*
bringing to an end its short and insubstantial life.

Consumed with guilt? Hardly. A frisson of imagined
Buddhism? Possibly. Would Mrs Moth and the kids
be at home waiting? Unlikely. It was either me or it.
For who is to say that my visitor wasn't a mutant killer
waiting for me to fall asleep before stuffing itself
down my throat and bringing to a suffocating end
this short and insubstantial life ... Do I hear thunder?

*   *   *

A second meteor, a host-carrier bearing aliens from
the Planet of the Moths, tears a hole in the damp taffeta
at the hem of the hills surrounding Black Torrington.
A soft rain still, but high above, a vellum moon.
In his room, the Tutor pours himself a large scotch,
guiltily wipes the smear of blood from the dust-jacket
and settles down, unaware of the avenging, impending swarm.

The death of John Berryman in slow motion

We open on a frozen river
(the spot where the poet has arranged to meet death).
   The whiteness is blinding.
   The glare hurts our eyes.

From somewhere above he jumps.
We see the shadow first
seeping into the ice
like a bruise. Thickening.

There is no sound but the wind
skulking beneath the bridge.

Now the body comes into shot.
Falling, blurred, a ragged bearskin.
The shadow opens its arms to greet it.

The wind is holding its breath.

We freeze frame at the moment of impact
(noting the look of surprise on the poet's face).
We then pan slowly upwards
to the grey Minnesota sky.

Fade to black.

Poem for a dead poet

He was a poet he was.
A proper poet.
He said things
that made you think
and said them nicely.
He saw things
that you or I
could never see
and saw them clearly.
He had a way
with language.
Images flocked around
him like birds,
St Francis, he was,
of the words. Words?
Why he could almost make 'em talk.

Big Ifs

To the mourners round his deathbed
William Blake was moved to say:
'Oh, if only I had taken
The time to write that play.'

Nor was William Shakespeare
Finally satisfied:
'I know there's a novel in me.'
(No sooner said than died.)

Beethoven in his darkest hour
Over and over he railed:
'If only I had learned to sing
Before my hearing failed.'

In the transept of St Paul's
Slumped Sir Christopher Wren:
'I'd give them something really good
If I could only do it again.'

Leonardo, Mozart, Rembrandt
Led sobbing through the Pearly Gates:
'If only I'd have . . .
I could have been one of the Greats.'

Children's Writer

John in the garden
Playing goodies and baddies

Janet in the bedroom
Playing mummies and daddies

Mummy in the kitchen
Washing and wiping

Daddy in the study
Stereotyping

Rabbit in Mixer Survives

A baby rabbit fell into a quarry's mixing machine yesterday and came out in the middle of a concrete block. But the rabbit still had the strength to dig its way free before the block set.

The tiny creature was scooped up with 30 tons of sand, then swirled and pounded through the complete mixing process. Mr Michael Hooper, the machine operator, found the rabbit shivering on top of the solid concrete block, its coat stiff with fragments. A hole from the middle of the block and paw marks showed the escape route.

Mr Reginald Denslow, manager of J. R. Pratt and Sons' quarry at Kilmington, near Axminster, Devon, said: 'This rabbit must have a lot more than nine lives to go through this machine. I just don't know how it avoided being suffocated, ground, squashed or cut in half.' With the 30 tons of sand, it was dropped into a weighing hopper and carried by conveyor to an overhead mixer where it was whirled around with gallons of water.

From there the rabbit was swept to a machine which hammers wet concrete into blocks by pressure of 100 lb per square inch. The rabbit was encased in a block eighteen inches long, nine inches high and six inches thick. Finally the blocks were ejected on to the floor to dry and the dazed rabbit clawed itself free. 'We cleaned him up, dried him by the electric fire, then he hopped away,' Mr Denslow said.
– *Daily Telegraph*

'Tell us a story Grandad'
The bunny rabbits implored
'About the block of concrete
Out of which you clawed.

'Tell every gory detail
Of how you struggled free
From the teeth of the Iron Monster
And swam through a quicksand sea.

'How you battled with the Humans
(And the part we like the most)
Your escape from the raging fire
When they held you there to roast.'

The old adventurer smiled
And waved a wrinkled paw
'All right children, settle down
I'll tell it just once more.'

His thin nose started twitching
Near-blind eyes began to flood
As the part that doesn't age
Drifted back to bunnyhood.

When spring was king of the seasons
And days were built to last
When thunder was merely thunder
Not a distant quarry blast.

How, leaving the warren one morning
Looking for somewhere to play,
He'd wandered far into the woods
And there had lost his way.

When suddenly without warning
The earth gave way, and he fell
Off the very edge of the world
Into the darkness of Hell.

Sharp as the colour of a carrot
On a new-born bunny's tongue
Was the picture he recalled
Of that day when he was young.

Trance-formed now by the memory
His voice was close to tears
But the story he was telling
Was falling on deaf ears.

There was giggling and nudging
And lots of 'Sssh – he'll hear'
For it was a trick, a game they played
Grown crueller with each year.

'Poor old Grandad' they tittered
As they one by one withdrew
'He's told it all so often
He now believes it's true.'

Young rabbits need fresh carrots
And his had long grown stale
So they left the old campaigner
Imprisoned in his tale.

Petrified by memories
Haunting ever strong
Encased in a block of time
Eighteen inches long.

*　*　*

Alone in a field in Devon
An old rabbit is sitting, talking,
When out of the wood, at the edge of the world,
A man with a gun comes walking.

Happy Ending

Out of the wood
at the edge of the world
a man with a gun
comes walking.
Feels not the sun
upon his face
nor hears a rabbit talking.

Over the edge
at the end of it all
the man stands
still as stone.
In his hands
the gun held
to his mouth like a microphone.

The rabbit
runs to safety
at the sudden cry
of pain.
As the man lets fly
a ferret
into the warren of his brain.

A Joy to be Old

It's a joy to be old.
Kids through school,
The dog dead and the car sold.

Worth their weight in gold,
Bus passes. Let asses rule.
It's a joy to be old.

The library when it's cold.
Immune from ridicule.
The dog dead and the car sold.

Time now to be bold.
Skinnydipping in the pool.
It's a joy to be old.

Death cannot be cajoled.
No rewinding the spool.
The dog dead and the car sold.

Don't have your fortune told.
Have fun playing the fool.
It's a joy to be old.
The dog dead and the car sold.

In Good Spirits

This icy winter's morning
I rise in good spirits.

On all fours I exhale
a long white breath
that hangs in the air
like a shimmering rope.

Under which, with arms akimbo
and eyes ablaze, I dance the limbo.

Nothing Ventured

Nothing ventured
I rise from my hangover
And take a walk along the towpath.

The wind is acting plain silly
And the sky, having nobody to answer to
Is all over the place.

The Thames (as it likes to be called)
Gives a passable impersonation of a river
But I remain unimpressed.

Suddenly in front of me, a woman.
We are walking at the same pace.
Lest she thinks I'm following her, I quicken mine.

She quickens hers. I break into a run.
So does she. It's looking bad now.
I'm gaining on her. God, what happens

When I catch up? Luckily, she trips
And sprawls headlong into a bed of nettles.
I sprint past with a cheery 'Hello'.

Out of sight, I leave the path and scramble
Down to the water's edge, where I stretch out
And pretend to be a body washed ashore.

There is something very comforting
About being a corpse. My cares float away
Like non-biodegradable bottles.

A cox crows. The crew slams on its oars
And a rowing boat rises out of the water
To teeter on splintering legs like a drunken tsetse fly.

Before it can be disentangled
And put into reverse, a miracle: Lazarus risen,
Is up and away along the towpath.

Near Hammersmith Bridge, the trainer
Is on the other foot, as a hooded figure,
Face in shadow, comes pounding towards me.

A jogger? A mugger?
A mugger whose hobby is jogging? Vice-versa?
(Why do such men always have two g's?)

I search in vain for a bed of nettles.
No need. She sprints past with a cheery 'Hello'.
I recognize the aromatherapist from Number 34.

* * *

Waiting beneath the bridge for my breath
To catch up, I hear a cry. A figure is leaning
Out over the river, one hand on the rail.

His screaming is sucked into the slipstream
Of roaring traffic. On the walkway, pedestrians
Hurry past like Bad Samaritans.

I break into a sweat and run,
Simultaneously. 'Hold on,' I cry, 'hold on.'
Galvanized, I'm up the stairs and at his side.

The would-be suicide is a man in his late twenties,
His thin frame shuddering with despair,
His eyes, clenched tattoos: HATE, HATE.

My opening gambit is the tried and trusted:
'Don't jump!' He walks straight into the cliché-trap.
'Leave me alone, I want to end it all.'

I ask him why? 'My wife has left me.'
My tone is sympathetic. 'That's sad,
But it's not the end of the world.'

'And I'm out of work and homeless.'
'It could be worse,' I say, and taking his arm
Firmly but reassuringly, move in close.

'If you think you're hard done by
You should hear what I've been through.
Suffering? I'll tell you about suffering.'

We are joined by a man in a blue uniform.
'I can handle this,' I snarl.
'You get back to your parking tickets.'

He turns out to be a major
In the Salvation Army, so I relent
And let him share the intimacy of the moment.

I explain the loneliness that is for ever
The fate of the true artist,
The icy coldness that grips the heart.

The black holes of infinite despair
Through which the sensitive spirit must pass.
The seasons in Hell. The flowers of Evil.

*   *   *

The tide was turning and a full moon rising
As I lighted upon the existentialist nightmare,
The chaos within that gives birth to the dancing star.

I was illustrating the perpetual angst and ennui
With a recent poem, when the would-be suicide
jumped – (First)

The Sally Army officer, four stanzas later.
I had done my best. I dried my tears,
Crossed the road and headed west.

On the way home, needless to say, it rained.
My hangover welcomed me with open arms.
Nothing gained.

Days

What I admire most about days
Is their immaculate sense of timing.

They appear
inevitably
at first light

Eke
themselves out slowly
over noon

Then edge
surefootedly
toward evening

To bow out
at the very soupçon
of darkness.

Spot on cue, every time.

Bees Cannot Fly

Bees cannot fly, scientists have proved it.
It is all to do with wingspan and body weight.
Aerodynamically incapable of sustained flight,
Bees simply cannot fly. And yet they do.

There's one there, unaware of its dodgy ratios,
A noisy bubble, a helium-filled steamroller.
Fat and proud of it, buzzing around the garden
As if it were the last day of the spring sales.

Trying on all the brightest flowers, squeezing itself
Into frilly numbers three sizes too small.
Bees can fly, there's no need to prove it. And sting.
When stung, do scientists refuse to believe it?

The Death of Poetry

The fallen leaves this morning
are in a silly mood.
Dancing and leapfrogging
they chase eachother down the road.

No, that's not true.
Leaves don't have moods.
Unable to dance or play organised games,
what you see is merely dead matter.

Then it's the wind bringing them to life!
Full of mischief, it races along the pavement
tugging at scarves, knocking off hats,
whistling as it goes.

No, that's not true either.
The wind doesn't have feelings. Inanimate,
it's a force of nature, as simple as that.
Wind is just air on the move.

Then it must be the sun smiling down on us!
Or the moon!
Yes, the moon who knows all our secrets,
dreaming in her star-filled chamber.

Boiling gas. Frozen rock.
Put away your pen. Close your book.

Here I Am

Here I am
getting on for seventy
and never having gone to work in ladies' underwear

Never run naked at night in the rain
Made love to a girl I'd just met on a plane

At that awkward age now between birth and death
I think of all the outrages unperpetrated
opportunities missed

The dragons unchased
The maidens unkissed
The wines still untasted
The oceans uncrossed
The fantasies wasted
The mad urges lost

Here I am
as old as Methuselah
was when he was my age
and never having stepped outside for a fight

Crossed on red, pissed on rosé (or white)
Pretty dull for a poet, I suppose, eh? Quite.

Crazy Bastard

I have always enjoyed the company of extroverts.
Wild-eyed men who would go too far
Up to the edge, and beyond. Mad, bad women.

Overcautious, me. Sensible shoes and a scarf
Tucked in. Fresh fruit and plenty of sleep.
If the sign said, 'Keep off', then off is where I'd keep.

*   *   *

Midsummer's eve in the sixties.
On a moonlit beach in Devon we sit around a fire
Drinking wine and cider. Someone strumming a guitar.

Suddenly, a girl strips off and runs into the sea.
Everybody follows suit, a whoop of flickering nakedness
Hot gold into cold silver.   Far out.

Not wanting to be last in I unbutton my jeans.
Then pause. Someone had better stay behind
And keep my eye on the clothes. Common sense.

I throw another piece of driftwood onto the fire
Above the crackle listen to the screams and the laughter
Take a long untroubled swig of scrumpy. Crazy bastard.

Perfume

I lack amongst other things a keen sense of smell.
Coffee I have no problem with. It leads me
by the nose into the kitchen each morning
before vanishing at first sip.

And cheap scent? Ah, bonsoir!
How many lamp-posts have I
almost walked into, senses blindfolded,
lost in the misdemeanours of time?

At twenty paces I can sniff the difference
between a vindaloo and a coq au vin.
Weak at the knees, I will answer
the siren call of onions sizzling,

Sent reeling, punch-drunk on garlic.
No, it's the subtleties that I miss.
Flowers. Those free gifts laid out
on Mother Nature's perfume counter.

Sad but true, roses smell red to me
(even white ones). Violets blue.
Everything in the garden, though lovely,
might as well be cling-filmed.

If I close my eyes and you hold up
a bloom, freshly picked, moist with dew,
I smell nothing. Your fingers perhaps?
Oil of Ulay? Nail varnish?

Then describe in loving detail its pinkness,
the glowing intensity of its petals,
and I will feel its warm breath upon me,
the distinctive scent of its colour.

Those flowers you left in the bedroom
a tangle of rainbows spilling from the vase.
Gorgeous. I turn off the light.
Take a deep breath. Smell only darkness.

5-star

The Mandarin Hotel, Jakarta.
5-star, bordering on the Milky Way.
Bathrobes a polar bear would kill for,
slippers I slide about in still.
A bowl with fruit so exotic,
you need a licence to peel
and instructions on how to eat.
A bed as big as this room.

Attached to a cellophaned bouquet of flowers
that looks too dangerous to unwrap,
a card from the Hotel Manager
who welcomes me (misspelling my name).
He telephones: Could we be photographed
together for the Hotel Magazine?
Puzzled, flattered and vaguely disquieted,
I agree. Within minutes
I am holding a glass of champagne,
his arm around my shoulder,
flicking through my limited series of smiles.

Then the inevitable: I am not
who he thought I was. I am not
who I am supposed to be.
He laughs it off, apologizes, and leaves,
taking the rest of the champagne with him.

I walk out on to the balcony.
From the 37th floor the city seeps
towards the horizon like something spilled.
Something not nice. That might stain.

I go back inside. Examine my passport
and get out the photographs.
A couple who could be anybody
against a wall that could be anywhere.
A dog. Children smiling.

I unwrap the flowers. Open the maxi-bar.

Melting into the Foreground

Head down and it's into the hangover.
Last night was a night best forgotten.
(Did you really kiss a strange man on the forehead?)

At first you were fine.
Melting into the foreground.
Unassuming. A good listener.

But listeners are speakers
Gagged by shyness
And soon the wine has
Pushed its velvet fingers down your throat.

You should have left then. Got your coat.
But no. You had the Taste.
Your newfound gift of garbled tongue
Seemed far too good to waste.

Like a vacuum-cleaner on heat
You careered hither and thither
Sucking up the smithereens
Of half-digested chat.

When not providing the lulls in conversation
Your strangled banter
Stumbled on to disbelieving ears.

Girls braved your leering incoherences
Being too polite to mock
(Although your charm was halitoxic,
Your wit, wet sand in a sock).

When not fawning over the hostess
You were falling over the furniture
(Helped to your feet, I recall,
By the strange man with the forehead).

Gauche attempts to prise telephone numbers
From happily married ladies
Did not go unnoticed.

Nor did pocketing a bottle of Bacardi
When trying to leave
In the best coat you could find.

I'd lie low if I were you.
Stay at home for a year or two.
Take up painting. Do something ceramic.
Failing that, emigrate to somewhere Islamic.

The best of luck whatever you do.
I'm baling out, you're on your own.
Cockpit blazing, out of control,
Into the hangover. Head down.

After-dinner Speaker

Sitting around the table each evening
his wife and family pick nervously
at their food, dreading the sound
of the tapping of the knife against the glass
of the rapping of the spoon upon the table,
signalling that he will rise to his feet
and upstanding, speak for forty minutes.
An hour sometimes, if the wine kicks in.

How they look forward
to those nights when he's away,
at a conference, say, of managers or teachers.
And they don't have to listen
to those boring, yawning after-dinner speeches.

Half-term

Half-term holiday, family away
Half-wanting to go, half-wanting to stay
Stay in bed for half the day.

Half-read, half-listen to the radio
Half-think things through. Get up,
Half-dressed, half-wonder what to do.

Eat half a loaf, drink half a bottle
(Save the other half until later).
Other half rings up. Feel better.

Vague Assumptions

I assume that the fire started before
   the fire-brigade arrived
I assume that the neighbours did not put on pyjamas
   and nightdresses to go out into the street
I assume that the woman is not in hysterics
   because the policeman has his arms around her
I assume that the suicide note left by the arsonist
   will not be found among the ashes

I assume that the siren's wail has nothing to do
   with the unhappiness of the ambulance
I assume that continentals drive on the right
   because foreign cars have the steering-wheel on the left
I assume that wing mirrors are a godsend
   to angels who care about good grooming
I assume that to a piece of flying glass
   one eye is as good as another

I assume that if the sun wasn't there for the earth to revolve
    around there would be fewer package holidays
I assume that a suitcase becomes heavy
   only when lifted

I assume that water boils
   only when the bubbles tell it to
I assume that because the old lady died
   the operation to save her life as a baby had not been successful

I assume that the bundle of rags asleep in Harrods' doorway
   is not queueing for the January sales
I assume that the people waiting in line for the DSS to open
   do not work there
I assume that the people lying on the floor of the bank
   are not taking it easy
I assume that the hooded figure wielding a gun at the counter
   is not opening an account

I assume that to claim the reward
   one must hand over the kitten
I assume that the shopping-trolley on the beach
   has not been washed ashore from a deep-sea supermarket
I assume that to achieve wisdom
   one must arrive after the event
I assume that by the time you read this
   I will have written it.

Prayer to Saint Grobianus

The patron saint of coarse people

Intercede for us dear saint we beseech thee
    We fuzzdutties and cullions
    Dunderwhelps and trollybags
    Lobcocks and loobies.

On our behalf seek divine forgiveness for
    We puzzlepates and pigsconces
    Ninnyhammers and humgruffins
    Gossoons and clapperdudgeons.

Have pity on we poor wretched sinners
    We blatherskites and lopdoodles
    Lickspiggots and clinchpoops
    Quibberdicks and Quakebuttocks.

Free us from the sorrows of this world
And grant eternal happiness in the next
    We snollygosters and gundyguts
    Gongoozlers and groutheads
    Ploots, quoobs, lurds and swillbellies.

As it was in the beginning, is now, and ever shall be,
World without end. OK?

152

The Bright Side

Things are so bad
I am reduced to scraping
The outside of the barrel.

And yet, I do not despair.
In the yard there are many
Worse off than myself. (Well, four:

A one-eyed rat
A three-legged cat
A corpse and the lavatory door.)

The Unknown Worrier

Don't worry, I'll do it for you
I'm a therapist *manqué*
Let me be your worry beads
I'll tell your cares away

Should I chance to sit beside you
In a café or a park
And a cloud is hanging over
Groaning, heavy and dark

You can bet that when it's time to go
You'll have nothing on your mind
While I sit in the shadow
Of the cloud you left behind

Don't worry, I'll do it for you
Relax, I'll take the strain
Anxiety is my forte
I've got worry on the brain

The Wrong Beds

Life is a hospital ward, and the beds we are put in
are the ones we don't want to be in.
We'd get better sooner if put over by the window.
Or by the radiator, one could suffer easier there.

At night, the impatient soul dreams of faraway places.
The Aegean: all marble and light. Where, upon a beach
as flat as a map, you could bask in the sun like a lizard.

The Pole: where, bathing in darkness, you could watch
the sparks from Hell reflected in a sky of ice. The soul
could be happier anywhere than where it happens to be.

Anywhere but here. We take our medicine daily,
nod politely, and grumble occasionally.
But it is out of our hands. Always the wrong place.
We didn't make our beds, but we lie in them.

Bits of Me

When people ask: 'How are you?'
I say, 'Bits of me are fine.'
And they are. Lots of me I'd take
anywhere. Be proud to show off.

But it's the bits that can't be seen
that worry. The boys in the backroom
who never get introduced.
The ones with the Latin names

who grumble about the hours I keep
and bang on the ceiling
when I'm enjoying myself. The overseers.
The smug biders of time.

Over the years our lifestyles
have become incompatible.
We were never really suited
and now I think they want out.

One day, on cue, they'll down tools.
Then it's curtains for me. (Washable
plastic on three sides.) Post-op.
Pre-med. The bed nearest the door.

Enter cheerful staff nurse (Irish
preferably), 'And how are you today?'
(I see red.) Famous last words:
'Bits of me are fine.' On cue, dead.

The Health Forecast

Well, it's been a disappointing day
in most parts, has it not?
So, let's have a look at tomorrow's charts
and see what we've got.

Let's start with the head, where tonight
a depression centred over the brain
will lift. Dark clouds move away
and pain will be widespread but light.

Exposed areas around the neck and shoulders
will be cold (if not wearing a vest)
and there may be dandruff on high ground
especially in the west.

Further inland:
Tomorrow will begin with a terrible thirst.
Lungs will be cloudy at first,
in some places for most of the day,
and that fog in the throat
simply won't go away.
So keep well wrapped up, won't you?

For central areas the outlook is fairly bright
although the liver seems unsettled
after a heavy night,
and a belt of high pressure, if worn too tight,
may cause discomfort.

Further south it will be mainly dry
although showers are expected in private parts
and winds will be high,
reaching gale force incontinent.
Some thunder.

Around midnight, this heavy front
is expected to move in,
resulting in cyclonic highs
in and around the upper thighs.

Temperatures will rise
and knees may well seize up in the heat.
And as for the feet,
perspiration will be widespread
resulting in a sweaty bedspread.

And the outlook for the weak?
Not as good as for the strong, I'm afraid.
Goodnight.

In Vain

I like liposuction, I've had my lipo sucked.
No flab to grab on my abdomen
My buttocks neatly tucked.

Implants in my pectorals, wrinkles all erased
Nosejob and a hairpiece, both eyes doubleglazed.
Zits all zapped by laser, cheekbones smashed and reset.
But sadly, my days are numbered,
I'm up to my ears . . .
Remember how they used to stick out? . . . in debt.

(For in brackets here I'll mention
A certain *glandular* extension)
Penile, in fact, which increased my libido
Though senile I act like a beast
And the need, oh the greed,
Oh those nights of seedless passion!

Which will doubtless explain
The cardiovascular pain
And three-way bypass, alas, in vain.

Wearing pyjamas designed by Armani
A perfect body waiting to die.
Bewigged, butchered and bewildered
Am I,
        Am I,
                Am I.

M.I.L.T.

Blessed are the children and happy the spouses
Lucky the neighbours who everyday meet
Mothers In Leather Trousers

Pushing their buggies in T-shirts or blouses
Swish-swash hear them shimmying down the street
Blessed are the children and happy the spouses

Bricklayers' labourers stop building houses
Scaffolders, road-diggers, drivers compete
To whistle at Mothers In Leather Trousers

South Kensington ladies, Brummies and Scousers
Sisterhood of bottoms large or petite
Blessed are the children and happy the spouses

What a smooth and beautiful skin the cow's is
Especially when softened and buffed up a treat
By Mothers In Leather Trousers

What man hasn't turned and tripped over his feet?
Polished anthracite with the promise of heat
Blessed are the children and happy the spouses
Who live with Mothers In Leather Trousers.

My Divine Juggler

Jugglers, as you can imagine,
are great fun to be with.
Mine is.
Alert and ambidextrous,
rarely dropping an aitch or missing a trick,
head in the air, clear-eyed and smiling,
I'm mad for him.

No couch potato he.
After a hard day in the busy town square
he comes home to prepare supper.
Under the spotlight in the kitchen
he works the vegetables, eight at a time.
Spins plates, tosses pans.
In orbit, knives hiss with pleasure.

In the bathroom, ducks and deodorants
spring to life in his hands.
Loofahs loop-the-loop. A Ferris Wheel
of shower-caps and shampoo bottles.
Flannels paraglide, soaps and sponges
dance a perfumed fandango.
I would die for him.

He will be the perfect father, I know it.
In the maternity ward he arrived,
laden with champagne and flowers.
Matron gasped, midwives giggled,
other mothers marvelled as the newlyborn
went spinning through the air like startled planets:
Mars, Mercury, Jupiter. Our triplets.
My divine juggler.

Echoes Sound Afar

Halfway up the mountain it stops. Slips back.
Judders. Slips again. *'Scheisse!'* screams a Fräulein,
'Scheisse!' Word for word, you think exactly
the same in English. Two little maids in white dresses,
toting Prada bags, think the same in Japanese.
The wind rocks the cradle, but not gently.

No driver. No door handles on the inside.
Reassuringly there is a hammer for smashing
windows in case of emergency. But is this
an emergency, or just the run up to one?
Unsure of the etiquette, better wait until the carriage
bursts into flames or fills up with water.

'Scheisse!' It slides back down the track.
Stops. Slides again. Stops and sways dizzily.
The German girl is on the floor sobbing,
her husband unable to comfort her.
A Texan, the life and soul, makes a joke
about the Big Dipper, but nobody laughs.

A voice crackles over the tannoy. *Pardon?*
If it were writing it would be illegible.
Why are there no Italians on board? Obviously
they've heard the rumours. So what did it say?
'Help is on its way', or, 'Emergency, you fools!
The hammer, use the bloody hammer!'

A power failure. Your lives hang on a thread
(albeit a rusty metal one circa 1888). A winch
turns and the long haul up begins. You hold
your breath. Twenty metres. Stop. Shudder,
and a sickening fall for ten. A tooth being
slowly drawn out and then pushed back in.

Should the cable break the descent will not be
death defying. The view below is breathtaking
but you have no wish to be part of it. Like the
muzzle of a mincing machine, the station waits
to chew you up and spit out the gristly bits
into the silver kidney bowl that is Lake Como.

An hour and a half later the tug-of-war ends
and the passengers alight heavily. The Brits to seek
an explanation. The Americans to seek compensation.
The Germans to seek first aid, and the Japanese,
seemingly unfazed, to seek a little shop that sells
snow-globes and model funicular railway sets.

Defying Gravity

Gravity is one of the oldest tricks in the book.
Let go of the book and it abseils to the ground
As if, at the centre of the earth, spins a giant yo-yo
To which everything is attached by an invisible string.

Tear out a page of the book and make an aeroplane.
Launch it. For an instant it seems that you have fashioned
A shape that can outwit air, that has slipped the knot.
But no. The earth turns, the winch tightens, it is wound in.

One of my closest friends is, at the time of writing,
Attempting to defy gravity, and will surely succeed.
Eighteen months ago he was playing rugby,
Now, seven stones lighter, his wife carries him aw-

Kwardly from room to room. Arranges him gently
Upon the sofa for the visitors. 'How are things?'
Asks one, not wanting to know. Pause. 'Not too bad.'
(Open brackets. Condition inoperable. Close brackets.)

Soon now, the man that I love (not the armful of bones)
Will defy gravity. Freeing himself from the tackle
He will sidestep the opposition and streak down the wing
Towards a dimension as yet unimagined.

Back where the strings are attached there will be a service
And homage paid to the giant yo-yo. A box of left-overs
Will be lowered into a space on loan from the clay.
Then, weighted down, the living will walk wearily away.

The Man in the Moon

On the edge of the jumping-off place I stood
Below me, the lake
Beyond that, the dark wood
And above, a night-sky that roared.

I picked a space between two stars
Held out my arms, and soared.

*   *   *

The journey lasted not half a minute
There is a moon reflected in the lake
You will find me in it.

Sad Music

We fall to the earth like leaves
Lives as brief as footprints in snow
No words express the grief we feel
I feel I cannot let her go.

For she is everywhere.
Walking on the windswept beach
Talking in the sunlit square.
Next to me in the car
I see her sitting there.

At night she dreams me
and in the morning the sun does not rise.
My life is as thin as the wind
And I am done with counting stars.

She is gone she is gone.
I am her sad music, and I play on, and on, and on.

The Trouble with Snowmen

'The trouble with snowmen,'
Said my father one year
'They are no sooner made
Than they just disappear.

I'll build you a snowman
And I'll build it to last
Add sand and cement
And then have it cast.

And so every winter,'
He went on to explain
'You shall have a snowman
Be it sunshine or rain.'

   * * *

And that snowman still stands
Though my father is gone
Out there in the garden
Like an unmarked gravestone.

Staring up at the house
Gross and misshapen
As if waiting for something
Bad to happen.

For as the years pass
And I grow older
When summers seem short
And winters colder.

The snowmen I envy
As I watch children play
Are the ones that are made
And then fade away.

Everyday Eclipses

The hamburger flipped across the face of the bun
The frisbee winning the race against its own shadow
The cricket ball dropping for six in front of the church clock
On a golden plate, a host of communion wafers
The brown contact lens sliding across the blue iris
The palming of small change
Everyday eclipses.

Out of the frying pan, the tossed pancake orbits
    the Chinese lampshade
The water bucket echoing into the well
The black, snookering the cue ball against the green baize
The winning putt on the eighteenth
The tiddlywink twinkling toward the tiddlycup
Everyday eclipses.

Neck and neck in the hot-air balloon race
Holding up her sign, the lollipop lady blots out
    the Belisha beacon
The foaming tankard thumped onto the beermat
The plug into the plughole
In the fruit bowl, the orange rolls in front of the peach
Every day eclipses another day.

Goodbye bald patch, Hello yarmulke
A sombrero tossed into the bullring
Leading the parade, the big bass drum, we hear cymbals
    but cannot see them
One eclipse eclipses another eclipse.

To the cold, white face, the oxygen mask
But too late
One death eclipses another death.

The baby's head, the mother's breast
The open O of the mouth seeking the warm O of the nipple
One birth eclipses another birth
Everyday eclipses.

Bearhugs

Whenever my sons call round we hug each other.
Bearhugs. Both bigger than me and stronger
They lift me off my feet, crushing the life out of me.

They smell of oil paint and aftershave, of beer
Sometimes and tobacco, and of women
Whose memory they seem reluctant to wash away.

They haven't lived with me for years,
Since they were tiny, and so each visit
Is an assessment, a reassurance of love unspoken.

I look for some resemblance to my family.
Seize on an expression, a lifted eyebrow,
A tilt of the head, but cannot see myself.

Though like each other, they are not like me.
But I can see in them something of my father.
Uncles, home on leave during the war.

At three or four, I loved those straightbacked men
Towering above me, smiling and confident.
The whole world before them. Or so it seemed.

I look at my boys, slouched in armchairs
They have outgrown. Imagine Tom in army uniform
And Finn in air force blue. Time is up.

Bearhugs. They lift me off my feet
And fifty years fall away. One son
After another, crushing the life into me.

Just Passing

Just passing, I spot you through the railings.
You don't see me. Why should you?
Outside the gates, I am out of your orbit.

Break-time for Infants and first-year Juniors
and the playground is a microcosmos:
planets, asteroids, molecules, chromosomes.

Constellations swirling, a genetic whirlpool
Worlds within worlds. A Russian doll
of universes bursting at each seam.

Here and there, some semblance of order
as those who would benefit from rules
are already seeking to impose them.

Not yet having to make sense of it all
you are in tune with chaos, at its centre.
Third son lucky, at play, oblivious of railings.

I try and catch your eye. To no avail.
Wave goodbye anyway, and pocketing
my notebook, move on. Someday we must talk.

Who are These Men?

Who are these men who would do you harm?
Not the mad-eyed who grumble at pavements
Banged up in a cell with childhood ghosts

Who shout suddenly and frighten you. Not they.
The men who would do you harm have gentle voices
Have practised their smiles in front of mirrors.

Disturbed as children, they are disturbed by them.
Obsessed. They wear kindness like a carapace
Day-dreaming up ways of cajoling you into the car.

Unattended, they are devices impatient
To explode. Ignore the helping hand
It will clench. Beware the lap, it is a trapdoor.

They are the spies in our midst. In the park,
Outside the playground, they watch and wait.
Given half a chance, love, they would take you

Undo you. Break you into a million pieces.
Perhaps, in time, I would learn forgiveness.
Perhaps, in time, I would kill one.

Cinders

After the pantomime, carrying you back to the car
On the coldest night of the year
My coat, black leather, cracking in the wind.

Through the darkness we are guided by a star
It is the one the Good Fairy gave you
You clutch it tightly, your magic wand.

And I clutch you tightly for fear you blow away
For fear you grow up too soon and – suddenly,
I almost slip, so take it steady down the hill.

Hunched against the wind and hobbling
I could be mistaken for your grandfather
And sensing this, I hold you tighter still.

Knowing that I will never see you dressed for the Ball
Be on hand to warn you against Prince Charmings
And the happy ever afters of pantomime.

On reaching the car I put you into the baby seat
And fumble with straps I have yet to master
Thinking, if only there were more time. More time.

You are crying now. Where is your wand?
Oh no. I can't face going back for it
Let some kid find it in tomorrow's snow.

Waiting in the wings, the witching hour.
Already the car is charging. Smells sweet
Of ripening seed. We must go. We must go.

Monstrance

He is neither big nor strong
But his four-year-old thinks he is

She runs towards him, arms outstretched
And is lifted up into the sky

Five times a week in Little Suburbia
He blazes like a tree

The Way Things Are

No, the candle is not crying, it cannot feel pain.
Even telescopes, like the rest of us, grow bored.
Bubblegum will not make the hair soft and shiny.
The duller the imagination, the faster the car,
I am your father and this is the way things are.

When the sky is looking the other way,
do not enter the forest. No, the wind
is not caused by the rushing of clouds.
An excuse is as good a reason as any.
A lighthouse, launched, will not go far,
I am your father and this is the way things are.

No, old people do not walk slowly
because they have plenty of time.
Gardening books when buried will not flower.
Though lightly worn, a crown may leave a scar,
I am your father and this is the way things are.

No, the red woolly hat has not been
put on the railing to keep it warm.
When one glove is missing, both are lost.
Today's craft fair is tomorrow's car boot sale.
The guitarist gently weeps, not the guitar,
I am your father and this is the way things are.

Pebbles work best without batteries.
The deckchair will fail as a unit of currency.
Even though your shadow is shortening
it does not mean you are growing smaller.
Moonbeams sadly, will not survive in a jar,
I am your father and this is the way things are.

For centuries the bullet remained quietly confident
that the gun would be invented.
A drowning surrealist will not appreciate
the concrete lifebelt.
No guarantee my last goodbye is au revoir,
I am your father and this is the way things are.

Do not become a prison-officer unless you know
what you're letting someone else in for.
The thrill of being a shower curtain will soon pall.
No trusting hand awaits the falling star,
I am your father, and I am sorry,
but this is the way things are.